THE CLAR~~ETS~~

A CLUB THAT DARED TO DREAM

First published in Great Britain in 2009 by
The Breedon Books Publishing Company Limited
Breedon House, 3 The Parker Centre,
Derby, DE21 4SZ.

ISBN: 978-1-85983-765-8

Printed and bound by Gutenberg Press Ltd, Malta.

THE CLARETS

A CLUB THAT DARED TO DREAM

Chris Boden

breedon **books**
PUBLISHING

CONTENTS

DEDICATION

With special thanks to
the players, officials and supporters
of Burnley Football Club.

FOREWORD

Ninety minutes that changed a town. Two days that will live in Burnley folklore forever. One season in which a football club dared to dream against all odds.

Burnley Football Club's promotion to the hallowed riches of the Premier League means everything to Burnley – a town that is football mad through and through.

For 48 hours in May 2009, Clarets supporters lived the dream. A club that had experienced the highs and lows of professional football found itself just 90 minutes from the Promised Land. The outcome of an already memorable season rested on just 90 minutes of football at the new Wembley Stadium.

Supporters had already tasted success in two amazing Cup campaigns. But they were just distant memories as the town of Burnley descended on the capital. Around 40,000 Clarets fans turned a little bit of North London into a sea of Claret and Blue – a feat that was repeated on home soil barely 24 hours later.

At appproximately 5pm on Monday 25 May 2009, the wait was over. The mighty Clarets had beaten Sheffield United 1–0 in the 2009 Championship Play-off Final. The Clarets were going up. The Clarets were a Premier League club.

This book seeks to capture in pictures the flavour and delight not just of that historic day, but also of the amazing celebrations that followed. Celebrations the like of which most Clarets fans had never seen before. A magical couple of days were rounded off with an open-top bus victory parade watched, astonishingly, by more people than had seen the match itself.

Young and old turned out bedecked in their beloved Claret and Blue, eager to see a glimpse of their conquering heroes. They were not disappointed. Led by manager Owen Coyle, elected to God-like status by adoring fans, the parade snaked its way past a sea of ecstatic faces towards its destination – Burnley Town Hall.

Burnley, a town that has taken more than its fair share of knocks in recent years, had a smile back on its face once again.

Enjoy this book. Revel in the success and take comfort in the belief that dreams can come true.

CHRIS DAGGETT
Editor, *Burnley Express*

Two fans in party mood.

A group of supporters on Wembley Way.

Outside the stadium.

Come on Burnley!

Claret colours well and truly on show.

Confidence was high in the build-up…

…after all, God was on Burnley's side.

Two young fans show what side they're on…

…while the little people of Habergham show their support

Fans travelled from far and wide…

…while the Quigley family made a special effort!

Burnley Express photographer (and Torquay fan) Andrew Smith shows his allegiance to the Burnley cause.

Eric Knowles, of *Antiques Roadshow* fame, shows his colours.

The Wembley scoreboard shows the task at hand…

…while the view inside the stadium was a joy to behold.

Supporters gather on Wembley Way…

…with one pair sporting some giant Robbie Blake pants!

One coach load of fans get ready for the trip.

Did this supporter have a premonition as regard the result?

More fans on Wembley Way…

…including some young Bertie Bee lookalikes.

Holland's Pies managing director Neil Court-Johnston (right) with chairman Barry Kilby.

The children of St Joseph's Park Hill Nursery.

(from left) Danny, Lynn and George Heys of Heys Butchers in Lyndhurst Road.

Children at Brunshaw Primary School.

Owen Coyle lines up with his players prior to kick-off.

The players conduct their pre-match huddle.

The fans look on as referee Mike Dean prepares to get the game underway.

Clarke Carlisle rises above Craig Beattie.

Robbie Blake tries to get the better of Kyle Walker.

Steven Thompson gets ahead of Chris Morgan.

Another solid clearance from Steven Caldwell.

Martin Paterson searches for an opening.

Steven Thompson bursts past Kyle Walker.

Kyle Walker makes a solid challenge on Chris Eagles.

Steven Thompson shows his determination to win the ball.

Michael Duff comes within inches of finding the target.

Brian Jensen goes in where it hurts to foil Matthew Kilgallon.

Greg Halford tries everything to stop Clarke Carlisle.

Joey Gudjonsson gets the better of Nick Montgomery.

Wade Elliott tries to repeat his goal heroics…

…and tussles with Stephen Quinn.

A strong header from Martin Paterson.

Burnley defend in numbers to thwart another Blades attack.

Robbie Blake at the heart of another attack.

Jamie Ward protests his innocence as he is given his marching orders..

Martin Paterson goes up against Matthew Kilgallon.

Wade Elliott looks on as United look to come forward.

Clarke Carlisle makes the ball his.

Craig Beattie is thwarted by Steven Caldwell.

Martin Paterson in the thick of the action.

Steven Thompson and Kyle Walker do battle.

The magical feet of Robbie Blake.

Wade Elliott prompts Burnley forward.

Christian Kalvenes holds off Kyle Walker's burst.

Wade Elliott skips through the United defence…

…after bursting through with a quick turn of pace.

Greg Halford fouls Clarke Carlisle.

Another strong header from Clarke Carlisle.

Steven Thompson makes the ball his.

David Cotterill and Christian Kalvenes do battle.

A quick burst from Steven Thompson.

Martin Paterson is thwarted by Nick Montgomery.

Chris McCann does battle with Greg Halford…

…before leading another Burnley attack.

Matthew Kilgallon tries his best to dispossess Steven Thompson.

Wade Elliott prompts Burnley forward.

The Blades defence puts pressure on Martin Paterson...

...who is again shadowed by Matthew Kilgallon.

Joey Gudjonsson heads a chance wide…

…and tussles with Chris Morgan.

Joey Gudjosson shakes off Nick Montgomery.

Kyle Naughton is alive to the danger as Martin Paterson looks to pounce.

Joey Gudjonsson is somehow denied by Nick Montgomery.

Kyle Walker keeps a close eye on Robbie Blake.

Wade Elliott urges the Clarets forward.

Joey Gudjonsson keeps possession.

Chris McCann receives treatment.

Wade Elliott takes aim…

…and fires.

GREAT Coke TASTE zero SUGAR
Coca-Cola zero
GREAT C
Coca-Cola CHAMPIONSHIP
PLAY OFF
RODRIGUEZ
19
Coca-Cola
COCA-COLA CH MP ONSHIP PLAY OFF WINNERS 200
BURNLEY F.C.

Owen Coyle contemplates possibly the longest six minutes of his life.

Robbie Blake prepares to reveal his legendary 'Bad Beat Bob' pants.

Alan Mahon (centre) cannot hide his emotions…

…much like his teammates.

Martin Paterson holds the trophy aloft.

Wade Elliott celebrates his winning goal…

…and salutes the crowd.

The celebrations are well underway.

Steven Caldwell and chairman Barry Kilby's wife, Sonya.

Brian Jensen holds the trophy aloft.

Graham Alexander congratulates Wade Elliott.

The delight on the faces of the players is clear.

Steven Caldwell milks the applause…

…and embraces Clarke Carlisle.

Brian Jensen leads the celebrations.

Owen Coyle is congratulated by chairman Barry Kilby…

…before receiving a kind word from Kilby's wife, Sonya.

Brian Jensen celebrates victory…

…and punches the air in delight.

Graham Alexander salutes the fans…

…as does Steven Caldwell.

Michael Duff at the final whistle.

The moment of celebration.

Steven Caldwell leads the squad….

…followed by the mastermind behind promotion, Owen Coyle.

Owen Coyle milks the congratulations.

Goal hero Wade Elliott with the match ball.

Dejection on the faces of the United players…

…as Burnley celebrate.

Robbie Blake shows his delight…

…which is clear for all to see.

A well deserved drink for Martin Paterson…

…before the squad celebrate the victory.

Owen Coyle with the trophy.

Wade Elliott holds the silverware aloft.

Kit man Daryl Bielby at the heart of the celebrations.

Chris Eagles celebrates with Steven Caldwell.

Clarke Carlisle and Owen Coyle share a laugh…

…before Carlisle parades the silverware.

Fans in full voice.

Claret flags are flying.

A sea of joyous Claret faces.

Burnley fans applaud at the final whistle.

Clarets march on Wembley…

…and emerge triumphant.

One happy Claret.

A supporter in full voice.

Kelvin Stuttard of the *Burnley Express* with the trophy.

A sea of Claret.

Burnley Express chief football writer Chris Boden with the trophy.

The Burnley end of Wembley erupts.

Burnley fans in full voice.

One man lending his support to the cause.

One Claret in party mood.

The moment of triumph.

Burnley fans savouring victory.

Steven Caldwell parades the trophy on the balcony of the town hall.

The players milk the applause aboard the open-top bus.

Supporters find a viewpoint on Centenary Way…

…as the bus continues on its journey.

Burnley Express chief football writer Chris Boden (centre) aboard the bus.

Steven Thompson leads the celebrations.

Fans pack Centenary Way as the parade passes by…

…and the players take it all in.

Supporters continue to fill the streets…

…with Steven Thompson making the most of the evening!

The bus continues on its journey.

A sea of claret greets the players…

…and continues…

...throughout the route.

The bus weaves its way through the crowds on Finsley Gate.

Owen Coyle with his daughter.

Robbie Blake salutes the crowd.

A wave to the supporters from Owen Coyle.

Chris Boden of the *Burnley Express* looks on.

Centenary Way braces itself for the tour party.

A young fan shows his support.

Fans line the roadside.

Burnley Express photographer Georgina Brewster.

Kelvin Stuttard of the *Burnley Express* catches the action on film.

Burnley Express photographer Andrew Smith.

The crowds continue to pack the streets.

Ben Parsons with his son, Joey.

Not a space to be had on Centenary Way…

…on either side of the carriageway.

The bus pulls up outside the town hall.

The crowd waits patiently…

…as Graham Alexander speaks to Alastair Campbell.

Wade Elliott is introduced to the crowd…

…and applauds the fans.

Owen Coyle on the town hall balcony…

…saluting the supporters.

Owen Coyle applauds the fans.

Chairman Barry Kilby speaks to Alastair Campbell.

Operational director Brendan Flood (left) with chairman Barry Kilby.

Club mascot Bertie Bee holds the trophy aloft.

The crowds continue to line the streets…

…as Robbie Blake appears on the balcony.

Robbie Blake continues to take the applause…

…before Steven Thompson kisses the trophy.

Alastair Campbell introduces Jay Rodriguez.

Chris Eagles applauds the supporters.

The crowds continue to be entertained…

…as Graham Alexander takes a memento of the day.

The banner says it all.

(from left) Christian Kalvenes, Steven Caldwell and Michael Duff.

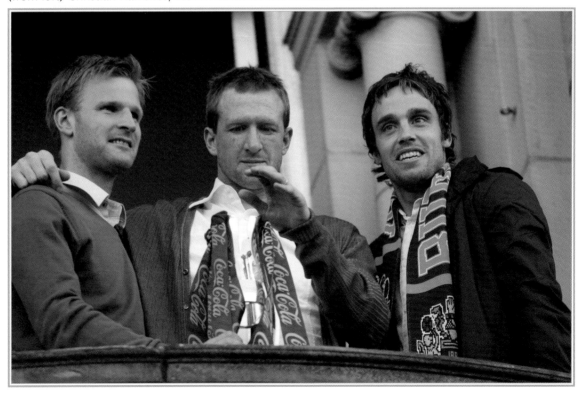

Michael Duff shows off his trademark dance…

…before Clarke Carlisle joins in!

Clarke Carlisle holds the trophy aloft.

Brian Jensen joins in with the celebrations.

(from left) Diego Penny, Brian Jensen and Alastair Campbell.

Burnley Express photographer Georgina Brewster.

The crowds are out in force on Manchester Road.

Brian Jensen aboard the bus.

Clarke Carlisle waves to the fans…

…while Steven Thompson continues to celebrate.

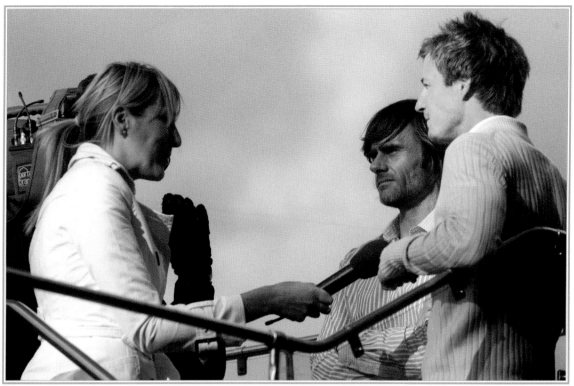

Graham Alexander and Wade Elliott are interviewed.

A flag is displayed proudly.

A giant pair of Robbie Blake's famous pants are displayed…

…while the T-shirt says it all.

Fans continue to line the streets.

Turf Moor catering manager Chris Gibson in party mood.

A section of proud Burnley fans…

…as the crowds gather outside the town hall.

Two supporters show their colours…

…as one man looks to take home memories of the day.

Steven Caldwell proudly parades the trophy.

Fans continue to celebrate…

…as a young supporter shows his colours.

The club's success brought fans from all over the world…

…and all were in voice.

**Championship
Play off Winners
TRANSDEV**

4005

TOUR
OFFICIAL
OF YORK

TRANSDEV

www.city-sightseeing.com
toplinetravel@aol.com

Information
01 904 65 55 85

The Clarets are g-Owen up!

Fans remain in full voice.

Supporters follow the bus route through the town…

…and set up camp outside the town hall.

Fans take their places along the route…

…loving every minute of the occasion.

One fan sums up the club's achievements.

Two fans show their colours.

Burnley Express journalists Dan Black (far left) and Dominic Collis.

Photographers Andrew Smith (left) and Andy Ford.

The masses gather outside the town hall.

Fans continue to show their support.

A selection of the players' wives and girlfriends…

…as the players continue to soak up the atmosphere.

The *Burnley Express* sums up the occasion.